The Rejects

The
Rejects

by Nathan Aaseng

Lerner Publications Company
Minneapolis

To Carrie

Page one: A Lear jet flies over Monument Valley, Utah.

Page two: Experts thought Orville Redenbacher's popcorn cost too much, but today the name Redenbacher means popcorn to many people.

Library of Congress Cataloging-in-Publication Data

Aaseng, Nathan.
  The rejects.

  Includes index.
  Summary: Describes various companies that succeeded despite initial rejection and the certainty of "experts" that the product they offered would fail.
  1. Success in business—United States—Case studies—Juvenile literature. [1. Success in business] I. Title.
HF5386.A39 1989   338'.02'0973   88-2780
ISBN 0-8225-0677-7

Manufactured in the United States of America

1 2 3 4 5 6 7 8 9 10 98 97 96 95 94 93 92 91 90 89

Contents

Introduction

"THERE'S ALWAYS ROOM FOR JELL-O," according to General Foods' slogan for its popular gelatin dessert. This may be true today, but in the product's early days, almost no one made room for it, except in their trash cans.

The first gelatin dessert was patented by inventor Peter Cooper before the Civil War. Fifty years later, in 1895, a cough medicine manufacturer named Pearl Wait tried to get rich from an adaptation of Cooper's formula, which he called "Jell-O." Not even the catchy name could attract customers, though. After four years of frustration, Wait sold the product rights to Orator Woodward.

Woodward quickly discovered why Wait had been so eager to part with the product. As stacks of unsold Jell-O packages piled up in his warehouse,

Woodward offered to sell the entire Jell-O business to a plant supervisor for $35. The supervisor turned it down.

Just when Woodward was prepared to write off his investment as a total loss, consumers began to find room for Jell-O. Sales of the dessert increased, until by 1906 Woodward was selling nearly one million dollars' worth a year. The Jell-O Company eventually became part of the General Foods Corporation, and the dessert that no one wanted has since become a familiar dish in cafeterias and homes throughout the country.

Innovators, tinkerers, and creative thinkers have often met with the silence of rejection or the laughter of skeptics. The history books describe a long succession of people whose breakthroughs were greeted with scorn instead of applause. Galileo's discovery that the earth revolved around the sun was denounced by most people, who believed that the earth was at the center of the universe. Louis Pasteur pioneered the science of bacteriology. Yet many people in his time scoffed at the idea that the world was teeming with invisible beings, some of which could even cause diseases.

"Fulton's Folly" and "Seward's Folly" were nicknames pinned on the first steamship and the purchase of Alaska. It seemed incredible that Robert Fulton's newfangled steamboat could really move or that the "frozen waste" of Alaska could be worth millions of dollars.

Orator Woodward

In all these cases, a creative person was able to see something in the future that the majority of people could not see. Strong in number, the majority could laugh or ignore the person who seemed out of step with the rest of the world. When the future arrived, however, it was the innovator who laughed loudest.

As the story of Jell-O shows, rejection happens in the business world as well. This book tells the stories of companies and products that were scorned, ignored, or dismissed as hopeless ventures. In the beginning, their prospects were no brighter than those of Jell-O at the turn of the century.

But the creative people behind these businesses and products bounced back from rejection. They believed so deeply in the worth of their ideas that they could continue to work in the face of skepticism. As a result, the names Xerox, Birdseye, Orville Redenbacher, *Reader's Digest*, Monopoly, and others have become familiar companions today. These products and businesses have outlived the critics who said "It will never work."

An early Nabisco advertisement for graham crackers

The Cracker That Was Banned in Boston

Graham Cracker

In THE EARLY 19TH CENTURY, THE Reverend Sylvester Graham's ideas about food were often laughed at or ignored. Today, however, his attacks on processed food and his belief in a wholesome, natural diet would be accepted by a large audience. He would probably be a popular speaker and author promoting a simpler, cleaner, vegetarian life-style.

Unfortunately, Graham lived at the wrong time. Although some people looked up to him as an inspirational leader, many others thought he was a fool. Popular philosopher Ralph Waldo Emerson scornfully called him the "poet of bran bread and pumpkins." Bakers in the northeastern United States had worse names for him. But even as Graham's followers left him and his teachings were scoffed at, one of his products grew amazingly popular. The graham cracker, which once caused a near-riot among bakers, became a favorite snack, even among people who disliked "health food."

Sylvester Graham was born in 1794, in West Suffield, Connecticut. His father, the famous clergyman and doctor John Graham, was 74 years old at Sylvester's birth, and he died when the youngster was two. With 16 older brothers and sisters in the family, Sylvester was lost in the shuffle. He lived with various neighbors while growing up.

Sylvester Graham

His strong interest in diets and life-styles was due partly to his own illness. He had tuberculosis, and although he eventually recovered from it, his health was never good again. Sylvester was always searching for ways to improve his health. He never did any scientific research; he just based his ideas on what he observed. He noticed who was healthy and who was not, then tried to discover how the healthy people lived.

Before long, Graham, who worked as a preacher in New Jersey, had cataloged a list of dos and don'ts. Most of these rules concerned eating habits. Reverend Graham believed that much illness was caused by the use of meat, alcohol, and processed flour. He thought people would be healthier if they drank nothing but water and ate only vegetables (especially green ones), fresh fruit, and bread products made with whole wheat.

He recommended sleeping with windows open

Perhaps if Sylvester Graham were living today, he would build a factory to make graham products and attempt to sell his products across the country.

But in Graham's time, many products were still made by hand and sold only in a small area. The bakers who finally began baking graham crackers served only small, local groups of people. Large-scale businesses were not common.

In the 1830s, industrialization began to increase in the Eastern United States. **Industrialization** is the change from the manufacturing, or making, of articles at home to making them in the factory, and the replacement of hand labor by machines. It allowed for a huge increase in the production of many kinds of goods. After the Civil War, industrialization shaped the production of most U.S. goods. By the late 1800s, most articles were no longer produced by hand or for a small, local group, but were produced in large quantities for groups across the nation.

(even on the coldest winter nights), taking cold showers, using a hard mattress, wearing loose clothing, getting plenty of exercise, and avoiding tobacco. Graham also believed that cheerful good spirits and laughter at mealtime helped digestion and led to better health.

Reverend Graham had a remarkable gift for rousing an audience. Because of that and his firm opposition to alcohol, the Pennsylvania Temperance Society (a group opposed to the use of alcoholic beverages) signed him on in 1830. He began touring New England, lecturing on the evils of drink and tobacco. Gradually, however, he began to include his other theories in his speeches.

Graham's fiery messages attracted large followings in some towns. When he published a book in 1832 outlining his ideas, he became something of a celebrity. People who followed his strict diet were known as Grahamites. Some of his strongest supporters even lived together in small groups. The most famous of these groups was at Brook Farm, near Boston. There Graham won over such converts as Horace Greeley, who later became a powerful newspaper editor and a presidential candidate.

Other Grahamites followed Sylvester's advice in their own homes. By the mid-1830s, New England had many Grahamite boardinghouses and health resorts. Several hotels in Boston and New York even offered special Grahamite tables at which only salad, greens, whole wheat bread, fruits, and nuts were served.

In the 1830s, bread was baked by hand, a few loaves at a time, and sold only locally.

Most people, however, still thought Graham's ideas were ridiculous. Newspaper editorials denounced him. But it was the bakers whom he angered most.

The bakers made many of the "unhealthy" processed products that the preacher spoke against. To get away from these foods, Graham had created his own recipes using whole grain. One of his recipes was for a kind of cracker that he had first promoted in 1829. Made from red winter wheat with tiny fragments of the whole grain spread throughout the dough, it had a pleasant crunch to it. With molasses added as a sweetener, the cracker became popular with Grahamites.

Bakers were often willing to ignore Graham's preachings. But in 1837, he published his "Treatise of Bread and Breadmaking." This work urged Grahamites to stop buying any kind of commercial bread and to bake their own instead. In the bakers' eyes, he had crossed the line from being an eccentric nuisance to being downright dangerous. They declared war on Graham and his whole wheat products.

A product is said to be **commercial** if it is sold for money.

That year, a large group of bakers broke up a lecture that Graham was giving at Armory Hall in Boston. They caused so much damage that both the Grahamites and the bakers were thrown out of the building. Graham rescheduled his lecture at the New Marlborough Hotel. The bakers then stormed that building, but men on the hotel's second floor dumped lime on the protestors and stopped the attack.

These attacks made everyone uneasy, and the bakers decided to try a different approach. Rather than reject all of Graham's ideas, they would use them. Bakers bought unsifted whole wheat flour, which became known as graham flour. They started to bake graham bread and graham crackers and used his name to sell them. Some of these products, especially the crackers, became well liked.

As graham crackers became more popular, Graham himself became less so. Grahamism faded in the late 1830s and died out completely in the next decade. Despite his efforts to discover the secrets of health, Sylvester Graham was not a good example of his own advice. He remained sickly all his life and died at the age of 57.

Though some of Graham's followers became disillusioned with their leader, the graham cracker gradually became a favorite food across the country. Now, after a century of neglect, many of Graham's dietary theories have become popular among health food advocates. Graham crackers, meanwhile, have gone over to the other side. Once scorned by bakers, they are now mass-produced using the processed wheat products that Sylvester Graham distrusted.

Today, most bread is mass-produced. **Mass production** is the production of goods in large quantities. Mass-produced items are each made alike. The jobs necessary to make the product are broken into small parts, and machines may do most of the work of people.

No Use Crying Over Spoiled Milk

Borden

Illustrations from an 1879 newspaper show different parts of the Borden condensed milk factory in New York.

Whⁱⁱⁱᵉ most people, and especially inventors, experience some rejection during their lives, Gail Borden practically made rejection his life's work. There must be few men who had so many grand ideas but failed so frequently and so publicly. Borden had his tombstone inscribed with the words, "I tried and failed, I tried again and again and succeeded." Borden was over 50 years old before one of his many schemes finally paid off.

Gail Borden was born on a farm near Norwich, New York, in 1801. He received only a year and a half of formal schooling, but he was rich in practical experience. After living on the farm for 14 years, he moved with his parents to Kentucky and then to the unsettled Indiana territory. Next he floated down the Mississippi River with his brother and joined the many pioneers who decided to settle in Texas. He picked up knowledge wherever he went and used it to support himself as a farmer, a cattle raiser, a surveyor, a school teacher, an editor, a real estate salesman, and a collector for the port of Galveston. Among his many accomplishments in his early years were drawing the first topographical map of Texas and coining the slogan "Remember the Alamo!"

Inventing was about the only occupation at which Borden was not successful. Unfortunately, it was also what he most liked to do. He designed a portable bathhouse so that women could change into and out of swim wear on the beach. He also built a wheel in the center of his dining room table so that dishes could easily be swung around to each diner.

Many of his ideas were so strange that they invited ridicule. The "Terraqueous Wagon," built with four wheels, sails, and a rudder so that it could travel on both land and water, nearly got him into deep trouble. After the passengers he had invited to sail on his trial run nearly drowned in the Gulf of Mexico, Borden abandoned the wagon. Another seagoing venture, a boat powered by steam-driven mechanical oars, never made it into production. The death of his wife from yellow fever in 1844 prompted him to make plans to avoid an epidemic by housing Galveston townsfolk in a huge refrigerated building for the summer. Predictably, no one took him up on his kindly offer.

After hearing of Texas settlers who were often

Gail Borden

sick from eating spoiled food, Borden started experimenting with food preparation. In an effort to make a nutritious food that would keep for a long time, Borden boiled meat, filtered the resulting broth, and concentrated it by removing some of the water from it. This extract was then mixed with flour and baked. Not only was it nutritious, but it could be baked into a hard biscuit that would last a long time before spoiling.

It seemed that Borden had finally invented something worthwhile. His "flat meat biscuit" attracted the interest of the United States Army in 1850, and it was purchased by a number of explorers. There was, however, a huge problem with the meat biscuit: most people thought it tasted awful. The meat biscuit venture failed and Borden lost money.

Haggard and gaunt, looking old beyond his years, Gail Borden stubbornly clung to his ill-fated inventing hobby. Though he had lost nearly all his money in the meat biscuit disaster, he began working on a way to condense milk.

Borden became interested in milk during an ocean voyage home from London. Rough seas made the ship's cows too sick to give milk, and Borden was haunted by the cries of hungry young children. Babies got sick from drinking contaminated milk.

Borden wanted to find a way to keep milk safe and wholesome over a long period of time. From his work with the meat biscuit, he knew that food products lasted longer when water was removed from them. Working in a friend's basement laboratory in Brooklyn, New York, Borden at first tried removing the water from milk by boiling it. That process worked for condensing meat extract, but it left the milk with a strong burnt taste.

By this time, Borden was too poor to support his family, so he sent them to live with relatives in upstate New York. While visiting them, he happened to stop at a Shaker colony (a religious sect). He watched these self-sufficient people boil fruit and maple syrup in airtight vacuum pans. The substances boiled at a much lower temperature in the vacuum pans than they would have boiled in the open air. Borden borrowed this idea, and also one of the copper pans, to boil milk without giving it a burnt taste.

By 1853 he had achieved a good-tasting, long-lasting product, and he applied for a patent on his process. So close to success at last, Borden ran into a barrier. The U.S. Patent Office rejected his application. Borden applied two more times and was again rejected. He was told that others had already invented ways of condensing milk and he had simply copied their ideas. The patent office also said that his process did not work.

After three frustrating years, two of Borden's friends made a scientific study of condensed milk processes and presented the results to the patent authorities. Based on their evidence that Borden's process was unique, Borden finally was awarded a patent on August 19, 1856.

As Gail Borden discovered, getting a patent is not always easy. A **patent** is the exclusive right to own, use, and dispose of an invention. If you invent something, you can apply for a patent, but the invention must meet three requirements to receive the patent. First, the invention must be new—no one else can have invented something similar. Second, the invention must be useful—not frivolous or harmful. Third, it must not be obvious; it cannot be something that anyone could easily invent.

When Gail Borden visited a Shaker village in New Lebanon, New York, in 1853 (above, *a Shaker meeting at Sabbathday Lake, Maine, in 1885*), *he learned of the vacuum pan* (below), *which he then used to make condensed milk.*

The long ordeal of rejection, however, was still not over. His poor record in business and his threadbare, ill-fitting clothes did not inspire investors' confidence. Borden had to beg the money from a wealthy friend. The money wasn't enough, though. Just a few months after setting up his business in an empty carriage factory in Wolcottville, Connecticut, the 55-year-old inventor was forced to shut it down. Farmers had no more confidence in him than anyone else did, and they refused to sell milk to him on credit.

Borden tried again, setting up the New York Condensed Milk Company in Burrville, Connecticut, in 1857. Once more, he ran into many financial problems. While riding a train to New York, however, he happened to meet a New York banker named Jeremiah Milbank. This chance meeting signaled a change in Borden's luck. Not only did Milbank give him a large loan, but a New York newspaper ran a story describing the fine quality of Borden's product.

From then on, sales rose. In 1859 the company sold $48,000 worth of condensed milk. Two years later, the U.S. Army placed a large order for its Civil War troops. Gail Borden, beaten and battered by ridicule, poverty, and ill luck for most of his life, triumphed in the end. His New York Condensed Milk Company was renamed in his honor in 1899, long after his death. (He died in 1874.) By then Borden products could be found on food shelves throughout the country.

From 1889 to 1903, Borden's Condensed Milk Company was headquartered in this New York City building.

The Secondhand Success

Reader's Digest

Like all of the entrepreneurs whose stories are told in this book, DeWitt Wallace showed a willingness to take risks. A willingness to take risks is an important characteristic of people who start their own businesses. Studies have found that successful entrepreneurs often have certain other traits. These include: a strong desire to be independent; the ability to learn from experience; self-motivation; self-confidence; a lot of energy; and the willingness to work hard.

PUBLISHERS REGULARLY COMPLAIN about receiving stacks of silly suggestions from people who think their ideas will be best-sellers. An idea submitted by a young sales promotion writer named DeWitt Wallace was certainly ridiculous, according to publishers in the early 1920s. At a time when it was tough to sell magazines filled with original stories, Wallace thought he could make money selling secondhand magazine stories.

Wallace's proposal ended up in the publishers' wastebaskets. But he believed he had a great idea, so it took more than laughter from "experts" to discourage him. Wallace began publishing a monthly selection of stories collected from other magazines. By the time of his death, Wallace's *Reader's Digest* had become the most successful periodical ever produced.

DeWitt Wallace was born in 1889 in St. Paul, Minnesota. Although his father was a minister and a college president, DeWitt was a born wheeler-dealer. As a boy, he tried a number of ambitious money-making ventures, from raising chickens to running an electrical repair service.

The academic world lured him away from these efforts long enough for him to attend the University of California. But after Wallace returned to St. Paul in 1912 to work for Webb Publishing Company, his business instincts resurfaced. His job at Webb was selling agricultural pamphlets. Wallace noticed the bewildering flood of free federal and state publications available for farmers. Reasoning that no farmer had time to read through all those pages, Wallace came up with the idea of organizing and combining the information. He sifted through the pamphlets himself and put together a 124-page booklet entitled *Getting the Most Out of Farming.* Along with a list of available publications, Wallace included a summary of what each publication was about.

DeWitt Wallace

Wallace sold his booklet to banks and stores, which then passed it on to their farming clients. He had found a great public need—more than 100,000 copies of the booklet were given out. That success inspired him to think of ways to use the same principle in other areas. He wondered if business-persons might be interested in a summary of business articles, or in a selection of shortened versions of articles. Perhaps as modern living got more hectic,

Wallace got his first taste of publishing when he worked at Webb Publishing Company in St. Paul, Minnesota.

the average reader would be interested in a digest of general magazine articles.

These thoughts were abruptly put out of Wallace's mind when the United States entered World War I and Wallace enlisted. He was seriously hurt in France and was taken to an army hospital to recover. The dull routine of hospital life left him plenty of time to read magazines and to think about his digest ideas. Most articles, he decided, could be shortened without losing their value. After a while he began to create shortened versions of the articles he was reading.

When he returned to St. Paul after the war, he practically camped out in the public library. In order to understand which topics were of long-lasting interest, he searched through old magazines for articles that were still newsworthy after 10 or 12 years.

In January 1920, Wallace gathered his condensed versions of 31 of the most fascinating articles he had found and traveled to the East Coast in search of a publisher. He offered to serve as editor of the magazine if someone else would publish it. That was a bold statement from an inexperienced newcomer to the business, and none of the publishers took him seriously. Even if he'd had experience, the idea of collecting secondhand articles ("cut and paste journalism," they called it) was laughable to publishers who cherished a reputation for quality. They also thought that a magazine could not attract an audience without the short fiction or the artwork that were popular features of other magazines.

While waiting for someone to take a chance on his scheme, Wallace worked in the publicity department of Westinghouse Electric. When he lost that job, he realized that if his project were ever to get off the ground, he could not just sit around and hope for a miracle.

In the fall of 1921, he married Lila Bell Acheson, a Canadian-born woman whom he had first met 10 years earlier in Tacoma, Washington. The two of them mailed out to prospective customers thousands of brochures announcing their planned magazine. Then they left on a honeymoon. When they returned, they found responses from 1,500 persons willing to pay the three-dollars-per-year subscription rate.

DeWitt Wallace had to obtain permission to reprint articles from other magazines in *Reader's Digest* because the articles were probably copyrighted. A **copyright** protects the use of literary and artistic expression. A copyright is similar to a patent, but a copyright protects the particular expression of ideas, not the ideas themselves. A copyright applies not to inventions but to artistic or expressive works, such as books, musical works, plays, computer programs, paintings, sculpture, movies, and magazine or newspaper articles. You have probably seen a copyright symbol before: ©. It means the work has been copyrighted.

Lila Acheson Wallace

Advertising is the presentation of ideas, goods, and services to the public; it is paid for by a sponsor. By not accepting advertisements in its early years, *Reader's Digest* was unusual among magazines. Most magazines —as well as television networks and radio stations— make almost all of their income from the revenues (money from sales) paid by advertisers.

Borrowing $5,000 from his family, DeWitt produced the first issue of *Reader's Digest* in February of 1922. The original articles were very much like the kinds of stories that the *Reader's Digest* prints today, including pieces on the prospects for the human race and information about the latest developments in poisonous gas.

The Wallaces worked in a windowless basement room in Greenwich Village, New York. They devoted themselves to producing "an article a day of lasting interest." Unable to afford subscriptions to the best magazines, they spent a great deal of time reading in the New York Public Library. When they found an article they wanted to use, they got permission from the publisher, copied the article, and shortened it.

By the end of the year, the unusual, pocket-sized magazine had attracted enough customers that the Wallaces could move to a better location. They chose Pleasantville, New York, where they had been married, and settled into a rented garage and pony shed.

DeWitt Wallace's knack of knowing which articles appealed to almost everyone continued to amaze the experts. *Reader's Digest* had more than 200,000 subscribers by 1929. As the magazine grew, changes were made. In 1933 the Wallaces began paying for the use of articles. A few years later, they started ordering original articles. In 1955 they broke a long-standing tradition and began allowing advertising in the *Digest*.

By the time DeWitt Wallace retired in 1973,

Reader's Digest was being sent worldwide in several languages to an estimated 100 million monthly readers! Its success came at a time when competition from television nearly destroyed general-interest magazines. No other mass-circulation, general-interest magazine survived, besides *Reader's Digest.*

Reader's Digest *head-quarters is in Pleasantville, New York, where DeWitt Wallace got married.*

A Cold Reception for Frozen Food

Birdseye

THE POPULAR BIRDSEYE BRAND NAME of frozen food products was not the invention of an advertising agency. It was the actual name of the quick-freeze inventor, Clarence Birdseye, although he pronounced it BIRDS-ee.

A superior product and a colorful name should have given Birdseye an edge in starting his own business. Unfortunately, Birdseye was not judged on his own merit. Early efforts at packaging frozen food had left a bad taste in the mouths of most consumers. By the time Birdseye came along, people had been disappointed so often by the claims of frozen food manufacturers that they had no appetite for frozen food. Birdseye's company floundered. It took the advertising clout of a much larger company to persuade people to try frozen food.

Clarence Birdseye was born in Gloucester, Massachusetts, in 1886. He came from a well-educated family; his grandfather was an inventor, and his father was a New York Supreme Court judge.

Birdseye demonstrated industriousness and a fascination with nature at an early age. He financed his college education by trapping rats and frogs and selling them to university laboratories. Following graduation from college, Birdseye continued working with animals. He spent most of the next decade roaming the harshest environments of North America. After spending many months collecting animals in the deserts of the southwestern United States, he traveled to Labrador, Canada, to obtain some silver foxes.

Although Birdseye changed careers many times, all of his jobs had to do with animals and the outdoors. At the age of 37, he wondered if he could use his exotic travels and experiences as a field naturalist, a fur trader, and a fishery inspector to begin a different and more profitable career. The experience that struck him as having the most potential was the Labrador expedition.

During that trip, which he had taken while he was in his late 20s, he and others braved winter storms and temperatures of -50°F (-46°C). With virtually no food to be found in the Arctic waste, the men lived off the fish they caught near the ocean. Birdseye watched as the Eskimo guides laid

Clarence Birdseye, shown in his office using a dictation machine, drew on his experience in the Arctic to invent a way to quick-freeze vegetables.

the fish out in the numbing cold to freeze. Familiar with the poor results of other attempts to preserve meat by freezing it, Birdseye was pleasantly surprised by the result. After weeks and even months of freezing, the fish kept its fresh flavor. Unlike commercial attempts at freezing, which left meat mushy in texture, this fish was juicy and meaty. Birdseye later noted the same effect when goose meat and caribou meat were frozen under similar bone-chilling conditions.

Birdseye checked with scientists to see if the abnormally cold conditions could be responsible for the improved quality. They told him that it was quite likely. During normal freezing, the cell structure of meat is damaged by ice crystals before the freezing process can be completed. Fish frozen quickly under the Labrador conditions would be thoroughly frozen before the ice crystals could ruin the flavor. Nutritionists also gave Birdseye encouraging news. Quick-freezing, he was told, could preserve nutrients that would be lost in conventional freezing methods.

Birdseye decided to borrow this Eskimo knowledge and adapt it to the commercial food business in the United States. Unfortunately, the technology for cheaply imitating Arctic conditions was not readily available in 1923. For more than a year, Birdseye patiently puttered with a number of processes. Finally, after a long series of disappointments, he wedged a package of fish between two metal surfaces that had been cooled to below zero. The metal

Marketing is the process of developing a product, determining how much it should cost, deciding how it should be sold, and making sure that people who want to buy the product can get it. One slogan describes marketing as "finding a need and filling it."

contact allowed for much faster freezing, and Birdseye was able to make a product far better than any commercial frozen food available at the time.

After experimenting with many kinds of foods, Birdseye felt confident enough to begin marketing frozen vegetables and fruit, as well as meat. After persuading financial backers of the quality of his product, he formed a company, General Seafoods Corporation, in 1924. Birdseye located his business in New York City to get the business advantages he needed. But he was too much of an outdoorsman to adapt to the urban life. He spent four hours each day commuting between the office and his farmhouse 80 miles outside the city.

Believing that the superior quality of his products would guarantee success, Birdseye had his company churn out huge amounts of frozen products. In 1926 he developed a quick-freezing machine that was 40 feet long and weighed 20 tons. With his new equipment, he was able to freeze and prepare for sale more than 1.5 million pounds of food by the winter of 1928.

But as weeks went by, he found that this 1.5 million pounds wasn't going anywhere. Consumers had heard too many promises in the past about frozen products that were supposed to be as good as fresh. Birdseye's claims of quality came too late for many who had tried frozen food and had disliked it. No amount of "evidence" could persuade them to try it again. Most grocers refused to invest money

General Foods Corporation installed freezers in grocery stores to promote Birdseye frozen food.

in the costly refrigeration equipment required to keep Birdseye's products in the stores. Those who did regretted it when their customers ignored the frozen products.

Birdseye could see that it would take a persistent effort, a massive advertising campaign, and more money than he could raise to change people's minds. His company was slipping into bankruptcy because of the large investment in equipment. His long commute each day also made it difficult to manage the shaky business. In 1929 he sold his business to the Postum Company for $22 million. Postum, which immediately changed its name to General Foods Corporation, named its frozen foods division after

Companies or individuals go into **bankruptcy** when they cannot pay their debts. You are in **debt** if you owe someone something. Debt is an obligation to pay something. Birdseye was nearing bankruptcy because he did not have enough money to pay the company that he bought his equipment from.

Birdseye, who continued to work for the company doing research. The pronunciation, however, was changed to the more picturesque "bird's eye."

General Foods could afford the years of financial sacrifice that it would take to change the terrible image of frozen food. The company began by building and installing, free of charge, special deep-freeze storage cases for 18 grocery stores in Springfield, Massachusetts. Then, during a 40-week campaign, sample products were given away. To insure quality over a wide delivery area, General Foods engineers designed the first super-insulated railroad cars.

Despite this costly effort, the public held out so stubbornly against frozen food that General Foods lost money on these products every year until 1937. Even then, its profits were marginal until World War II. Calculating that 20 million pounds of canned vegetables would use up 2,600 tons of valuable steel needed for the war effort, the United States government agreed to buy enormous amounts of frozen food. By the war's end, people had grown used to it. With its bad image finally buried, frozen food began to take over large sections of grocery stores. Over 30 years after his death in 1956, Clarence Birdseye's name remains on the labels of many popular frozen food products.

A 1941 advertisement for frozen peas

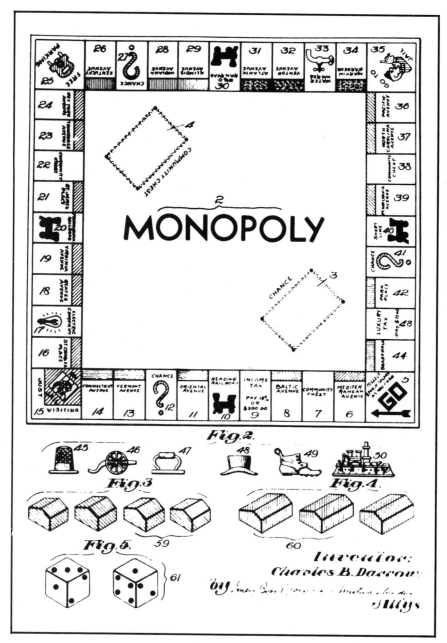

Illustration from Charles Darrow's patent for Monopoly

Everything You Don't Want in a Game

Monopoly

CHARLES B. DARROW MIGHT HAVE been happier with a standard, impersonal rejection letter than he was with the response he received from the Parker Brothers game company. Parker Brothers was polite enough to respond personally to his game proposal, but the response was terrible. The letter said there were dozens of reasons why Darrow's game would never sell. In the company's opinion, his real estate board game was a model for everything that a game *shouldn't* be.

Just months after making this judgment, though, Parker Brothers had to eat those words. If it hadn't, this manufacturer of many of the most popular games in the United States probably would not exist today.

Charles Darrow, of Germantown, Pennsylvania,

During the Depression, many people stood in line for hours to get free food.

was a typical victim of the Great Depression of the 1930s. He had been happily employed as a sales representative for a heating equipment firm when the economic disaster struck. Darrow lost his job in 1930 and spent many frustrating months looking for another one. Barely able to make ends meet, he lived with his pregnant wife and small child in a run-down old house. He found himself competing with other 40-year-old heads of households for odd jobs such as mowing lawns and shoveling snow off sidewalks.

The sudden plunge into poverty changed his goals.

During the 1930s, the United States suffered through a period called the **Great Depression**. In general, a depression is a period when production and consumption of goods and services slow down. It is a time marked by unemployment and business failures, and people do not have much money to live on.

The Great Depression of the 1930s followed the stock market crash of 1929. Economic growth in the 1920s had led many Americans to invest in **stocks,** or shares of ownership in companies. The value of stocks had soared as more and more people invested, but in late October, 1929, stock prices had dropped. Investors had panicked and sold stocks frantically. The "crash," as it was called, had resulted in drastically lowered stock prices.

The crash helped trigger the Great Depression. Following the crash, banks stopped giving many loans to businesses, and businesses cut back production. Millions of people lost their jobs, and poverty spread throughout the United States. By the early 1930s, the U.S. economy was paralyzed. At the height of the Depression, in 1933, about 13 million Americans were out of work. The Depression continued until 1941, when the U.S. entered World War II.

Instead of looking for a steady job, Darrow began to hunt for a way to achieve instant wealth. The surest way to get rich seemed to be to invent something. Darrow gave it his best shot, but the products he invented—a combination bat and ball and a simplified version of a scoring pad for bridge players —excited no one.

Then, according to popular legend, Darrow dreamed up the game that eventually made him rich: Monopoly. Darrow did patent the game—but he didn't invent it by himself. It might be more correct to say that he *discovered* the game.

The precursor of the Monopoly game was invented in 1904 by a woman named Elizabeth (Lizzie) Magie. The Landlord's Game, as she called it, allowed players to buy property and utilities and included "Go to Jail" and Park spaces.

Magie sold some copies of the game around the East Coast, but it didn't become popular. In 1924, she revised her game—adding a new "Monopoly" card, among other things—and offered it to Parker Brothers. The company turned it down. Although the game wasn't a commercial success, college students in Pennsylvania and other states liked to play it and it gradually made its way into people's homes. Improvements and refinements were made as more people played. By the mid-1920s, the game was known as "Monopoly."

At that time, the street names for the game's rental properties were taken from whatever town

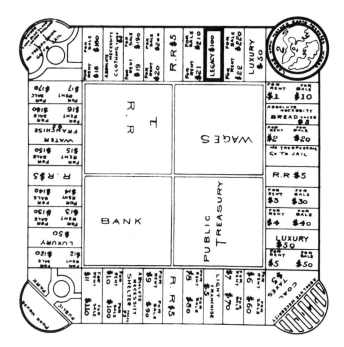

Lizzie Magie's "Landlord's Game" resembles the modern Monopoly game in many ways, as this patent illustration shows.

the game was being played in. The street names of the current Monopoly board—which come from Atlantic City, New Jersey—were given to the game by a player named Ruth Hoskins, who lived in Atlantic City.

Finally, one evening in 1933, an old classmate of Charles Darrow's wife brought a handmade copy of the game to Darrow's home. Darrow was completely taken with it. He decided to make his own Monopoly game.

Darrow carefully designed his own game board, using a piece of linoleum. He gave each series of spaces its own color, using paint samples from a nearby store. Darrow did not change the Atlantic

City street names. Like many others of his day, he envisioned that city as a kind of paradise. A few adjustments were needed. Atlantic City was served by three railroads, the Baltimore & Ohio, the Reading, and the Pennsylvania. Darrow wanted another railroad for the fourth side of his game board, so he borrowed a bus company's name—the Short Line.

Darrow spared no detail in making his game attractive. He typed the titles to the properties on cardboard squares and carved game pieces from scraps of wood.

At first Darrow was content to keep his fantasy business world for himself and a few friends. It took him an entire day to construct a single game set, and that would hardly make him rich quick. But those who played with him enjoyed the game so much that they begged him to make copies for them. Because he had so much free time on his hands, Darrow obliged them.

His friends played the game with their friends, who told still others about the game. Without spending a cent on advertising, Darrow found himself overwhelmed with orders. At first, he hired a printer to help him keep up with the demand. But when department stores and customers as far away as California sent in requests for Monopoly, Darrow realized that he might have discovered his road to wealth. It was time to make a decision: he had to either gamble on starting his own company or sell his game to an existing company.

While taking risks was fun in a game situation, a real-life risk was more serious. Rather than start a new company, Darrow approached Parker Brothers. This game company had been founded in 1883 by George Parker and his brother Charles. At 16, George had organized the company to manufacture and sell a game he invented called Banking. On the strength of that game, Parker Brothers built a good reputation for producing a variety of games. The Depression, however, had not left the company untouched. When Darrow offered Parker Brothers his game idea, sales were so low that the company was close to bankruptcy.

The company listened to Darrow's proposed game —and decided it was exactly what Parker Brothers did not need. The game experts told Darrow they found 52 reasons why his game would never sell! The object of the game was not simple enough for people to understand quickly how to play. The rules were long and complicated. Instead of moving toward an objective, players kept going around and around the board. Worst of all, the game could go on for hours, even days, before someone finally won.

Although it was a brutal rejection, Darrow had seen too much evidence of interest in the game to give up. The experts could say what they wanted to about his game, but people liked it and were buying it. Darrow took the risk of borrowing money to hire printers to do the manufacturing. Armed with 5,000 Monopoly sets, he concentrated on selling.

Charles Darrow brought Monopoly to Parker Brothers, but the company rejected the game. Undaunted, Darrow produced Monopoly himself and it became a success. Later Parker Brothers offered to buy the rights to the game, and Darrow achieved his dream of getting rich.

At first, it seemed he was better off not trying to sell the game. At the beginning of 1934, orders trailed off, and he sold fewer sets than expected. But people who played Monopoly spoke of it with such enthusiasm that orders began pouring in later that year. One store in Philadelphia alone ordered 5,000 sets.

An executive at Parker Brothers learned that Darrow was marketing his game on his own—with success. The executive realized that the company had been too hasty in its first judgment. The company swallowed its pride and bought the patent and rights to the game from Darrow in 1935, as well as the patents belonging to Lizzie Magie. Darrow's wish of becoming a millionaire was fulfilled. He retired early on a farm in Pennsylvania and never invented another game.

George Parker

The game that it had rejected pulled Parker Brothers from the edge of disaster. By February of 1936, the company had all it could do just to process the laundry baskets full of orders for Monopoly that came in from around the country. The plant was soon producing 20,000 sets a week. The game that was everything a game shouldn't be has become the largest-selling board game of all time.

From Zero to Xerox

Xerox

SOMETIMES IT SEEMS LIKE WE ARE surrounded by a sea of paper. The demand for information is so large that businesses, governments, schools, homes, mailboxes, and sanitary landfills are nearly buried under typewritten pages.

The machine most responsible for this abundance of written information can be found in the corners of business offices, post offices, and libraries. The photocopiers pioneered by Xerox are in almost constant use, spewing out millions of documents every day. It is hard to imagine how offices could function without them.

Fifty years ago, however, experts couldn't imagine these copy machines serving any useful purpose. No major producer of office equipment in the United States was interested in xerographic copy machines.

Only a tiny, failing company and a private research organization, figuring they had nothing to lose, dared to gamble on this new technology. The story of Chester Carlson and his marvelous invention is a prime example of how cloudy the business world's crystal ball can be.

Chester Carlson was born in Seattle, Washington, in 1906 and grew up in San Bernardino, California. His father, a barber, suffered from severe arthritis, and his mother was bedridden with tuberculosis. As the only child in the family, at the age of 14 Chester began working after school to help pay the bills.

Through one of his jobs, Carlson found the field of study that would change his life. A local printer for whom the teenager was working was getting rid of an old printing press. Carlson asked if he could have it as part of his pay, and the printer agreed.

Carlson, who was fascinated by chemistry, wanted to use the press to publish his own magazine for amateur chemistry fans. He printed only two issues, which, he later admitted, were not impressive. But through that experience, he learned about the printing process, and he began to think of ways to improve that process.

Printing was just a hobby, however, and Carlson soon became concerned with the serious matter of a career. His degree in physics from the California Institute of Technology would normally have given him his choice of jobs. Unfortunately, he was job-hunting during the Great Depression. Although he

A **nonprofit organization** is one which does not seek to make a profit. A company is said to make a **profit** when the money it earns from sales amounts to more than the cost of producing the goods or service. Some nonprofit organizations include the government, churches, schools, charities, and hospitals.

sent out more than 80 letters of application to firms around the country, Carlson received only two answers. He had to travel across the country to the Bell Telephone Laboratories in New York City to find work. Then, shortly after he arrived, he was laid off.

With his dream of a career in physics fading, Carlson had to take whatever job he could find. He ended up working in the office of a patent attorney. Carlson seemed to thrive on whatever task he was involved in, and he soon decided that he too would practice patent law. Used to hard work from his teen-age years, Carlson worked at the office during the day, went to law school in the evening, and studied in his spare time. After getting his law degree, he settled down to enjoy this higher-paying career.

But patent law had its problems. As manager of the patent department of a large firm, Carlson had trouble organizing his files. Patent procedures required that he file several copies of various detailed patent plans, yet his clients rarely gave him enough carbon copies. Photocopying each sheet was possible, but it was an expensive process involving photographic reproduction. The only other choice he had was to retype and redraw the originals, a time-consuming process and an easy way for mistakes to be made.

Carlson again found himself wondering about new ways of copying print. This time he started a serious search for an answer. Large companies working on the same problem were focusing their research efforts on conventional photographic methods. Carlson set off in an entirely different direction. Spending his evenings reading scientific journals at the New York Public Library, he studied every article he could find in the field of photoconductivity.

Following the lead of a Hungarian physicist named Paul Selenyi, he narrowed his search to the obscure science of electrophotography and began to conduct experiments in the kitchen of his apartment in Queens. He based his research on two facts: (1) positive and negative electrical charges are attracted to each other, and (2) some materials conduct electricity better when exposed to light. He thought of combining these two facts in a new way.

Carlson knew that he was on the verge of a whole new concept in copying. Best of all, there were no competitors. He realized, though, that at the rate he was going, he would never perfect his invention. By working only in his spare time with arthritic fingers on homemade equipment, he was letting the opportunity of a lifetime slip away. He therefore took the risk of using all his savings to rent a second-floor room above a bar in Astoria, New York. There he set up a laboratory and hired Otto Kornei, an unemployed physicist who had recently fled from Nazi Germany, to help run his experiments.

On October 22, 1938, the first electrophotographic copy was made. For the experiment, the note "10-22-38 ASTORIA" was printed in India ink on a

If Chester Carlson had been working for a large company while he was doing his experiments, he probably would have been part of a research and development department. Many companies spend large amounts of money on research and development. **Research** is investigation aimed at discovering new scientific knowledge. **Development** is the attempt to use new knowledge to make useful products or processes.

Chester Carlson recreates the first photocopy, which read simply "10-22-38 ASTORIA."

glass slide. Then the slide was laid on a plate coated with sulfur, a material that would conduct electricity when exposed to light. The plate had a positive electrical charge. Brief exposure to a bright light took away that positive charge everywhere but under the printing. Next, the slide was removed and a powder with a negative charge was sprinkled on the plate. The negative powder stuck to the positive area where the printing had been. When the loose powder was blown away, Carlson had a plate with a perfect image of "10-22-38 ASTORIA." It wasn't a copy of a paper original reproduced on paper—just a glass slide reproduced on a metal plate—but it was a first step.

After receiving a patent for developing his new process, Carlson found out that inventing it was much easier than selling it. From 1939 to 1944, Carlson knocked on the doors of companies most likely to be interested in his invention. None of them wanted any part of his process, and only a handful of them thought his idea even worth discussing.

Part of the problem was simply poor timing. With the nation involved in the Second World War, few businesses could spare the time or the money to manufacture an unproven, nonvital commercial product. In addition, Carlson's quiet, shy nature was hardly suited to sales.

Several times, the discouraged inventor was ready to admit that his patented invention was not the breakthrough he had claimed it was. He debated about giving up on the project altogether. Finally, he sought advice from Russell Dayton, a physicist he had met while working as a patent attorney. Dayton worked for a nonprofit research group in Columbus, Ohio, known as Battelle Memorial Institute. Dayton recognized that Carlson's concept might be of interest to the Battelle Development Corporation, a subsidiary that developed new inventions.

The Institute invited Carlson to its headquarters to demonstrate his invention. Battelle management

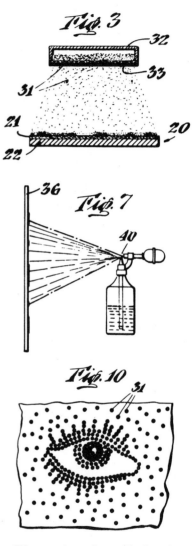

Illustrations from Carlson's patent for electrophotography

Royalty payments are payments a manufacturer makes to an inventor for each article sold that includes a device for which the inventor owns the patent. Under Carlson's agreement, he would receive a royalty payment for each copying machine sold.

and graphic arts specialists thought that the process looked "like a good research gamble." They also envisioned many uses in addition to office copying. So in October of 1944—six years after Carlson made his first electrophotographic image—Battelle signed a contract with Carlson to develop the project. Under the agreement, Battelle would financially support the development, as well as conduct research, in exchange for royalty payments once the technology was commercialized.

Battelle's graphic arts researchers enthusiastically embarked on the new project. They learned its basic principles and obtained a better understanding of what worked, what didn't, and why. Battelle's staff significantly advanced Carlson's crude invention. During these years the process also got a new name —*xerography*. It was a combination of Greek words meaning *dry writing*.

Meanwhile, a small company in Rochester, New York, looked at its financial situation and admitted the future was bleak. The Haloid Company, maker of photographic paper since 1906, was in trouble. The market for its paper was shrinking, and unless the firm could find a new product, it was doomed to failure.

During their search for something new, Haloid management came across an article in a technical magazine that described the achievements of unknown inventor Chester Carlson. After investigating Carlson's findings, they decided to risk the

Carlson, center, watches with a smile of pride as the first Xerox machine produced by the Haloid Company is set in motion.

entire company on the success of xerography. Haloid worked out an agreement with Battelle to continue development of the technology and then made additional refinements. In 1949 Haloid introduced its first Xerox machine. Although it demonstrated that the process of dry copying could work, it was far too crude to be of any widespread use. Besides being slow and messy, the copier was so complex it almost needed a physicist to run it.

Haloid did not give up. During the 1950s, the firm spent more money on improving its copying process than the company's entire earnings for that period. In 1959 the first office copy machine was tested and ready for the market. It proved to be well worth the wait and the effort. At the touch of a button, the machine could copy any page within seconds. That copier proved to be one of the most successful single products ever marketed.

For Carlson, xerography's commercial success turned a fantasy into reality and brought him a fortune. For Battelle, earnings from xerography enabled the modest-sized research institute to expand into many new fields and to grow into one of the world's leading technology development organizations. And Haloid's profits jumped from $2 million in 1959 to $22 million in 1963. In 1961 the company changed its name to the Xerox Corporation to better describe its business. Xerox has since grown into a multi-billion-dollar company, and its name has become a synonym for document copying.

It all happened because of a single dedicated inventor and two relatively unknown organizations that took a chance on a promising new technology that no one else wanted.

In 1961 the Haloid Company changed its name to the Xerox Corporation. Today, Xerox is one of the largest corporations in the United States.

The Little Plane That Could

Lear Jet

WHEN WILLIAM LEAR ANNOUNCED in 1963 that he was starting a new business to build small, inexpensive jets, aviation experts did not debate whether or not he would succeed. Their only arguments were over which part of Lear's proposal was the most ridiculous. It was clear to anyone who studied the industry that stripped-down jet planes wouldn't sell. And if such a plane did sell, it wouldn't matter—because no plane made the way Lear proposed could possibly fly. But even that point was hardly worth mentioning, because a jet based on Lear's ideas could not even be built on such a small scale.

It wasn't the first time Lear had been told his plans for some new project could not work. In 1963 the odds were stacked more highly than usual against him. Bill Lear backed up his claims by building the plane. Not only did it fly well, but it also sold well enough to change the way major corporations did business.

William Lear was an only child, born in 1902 in Hannibal, Missouri. After his parents divorced, he moved with his mother to Chicago. He spent much of his time alone, dreaming of being an inventor. Whenever he started a project, though, he had to stop halfway through for lack of money to finish the job. At the age of 12, he vowed to make enough money so that he would never be stopped from finishing anything again.

For Lear, school was something that just got in the way of his plans. He would often skip class and ride his bike along highways in search of stalled cars. He could usually fix any engine problem and, after charging a fee, would soon have the motorist back on the road. Following eighth grade, Lear quit school altogether to earn money as a mechanic. A determined lad with an abundance of confidence and energy, he left home at 16 and lied about his age to join the Navy. He then began to study radios.

Young Lear's life seemed to be one episode after another of dramatic success and failure. By the time he was 20, the electronics wizard was heading his own company, Quincy Radio Laboratories in Quincy, Illinois. By the age of 32, he had gone into and out of business several times, had amassed and lost a fortune, and was flat broke.

During that time, he had thought up several original ideas with far-reaching effects for the radio industry. It was Lear's brainstorm that had led to the production of the Majestic, the first popular, mass-produced radio for the home. It was also his idea to install radios in automobiles. Many objectors said a radio couldn't fit in a car and would be too distracting to drivers even if it did. But Lear had gone ahead and developed a practical radio and demonstrated its worth. Without financial backing, though, Lear had been forced to sell his idea to the Galvin Manufacturing Company, which later was renamed Motorola.

In the early 1930s, Lear struck off in a new direction —aviation. He had always been interested in airplanes, so interested that he had even worked without pay for a time as an airport mechanic in Chicago. Although his first attempt at piloting had ended with the plane flipping and his being thrown out the window, Lear had stuck with it and had purchased his own biplane.

Lear's aircraft radio

Starting from scratch, Lear began making aircraft radios in a small airport in Chicago. The future seemed promising, so he moved his operations to New York City. But in April 1934, three months after the move, Lear was out of business. In that short span of time, he had lost every cent he had made.

It seemed that the worse his situation, the more Lear was inspired to invent. His restless mind turned to aircraft problems, and he developed the Learo-scope, a navigational device that used radio signals to help pilots reach their destinations.

His next brainstorm was the development of a simple radio frequency amplifier. Unlike other amplifiers of the time, Lear's could be used by almost any radio set made. RCA made him a handsome offer for the amplifier, and Lear accepted the money to start yet another new company. In 1939 he made his boldest move yet. He formed Lear, Incorporated, in Grand Rapids, Michigan, to manufacture aircraft instruments.

The new company grew rapidly due to World War II defense contracts. In time, the firm employed more than 300 scientists and engineers and over 1,800 other employees. Among its successes were a revolutionary automatic piloting device for fighter pilots and several communication devices that were used in satellites beginning in the 1950s.

While on a business trip to Europe, Lear's attention was drawn to yet another project. He learned of an attempt by the Swiss to design a small-scale jet. Even though the project was shut down after two experimental planes had crashed, Lear was intrigued by the idea of a small, low-cost jet for business executives. His company's board of directors was not interested, however. They told him that such a plane could not be built.

Lear was not one to discuss whether or not something would work. "For crying out loud, try

The corporation has become the major form of business in the United States. Technically, a **corporation** is an association of individuals permitted by law to use a common name and to change its membership without ending the association. Most people think of a corporation as just a large company, though. Because starting a business requires a large sum of money, many people choose to form a corporation, or **incorporate**. By forming a corporation, people starting a new business may be able to raise large sums of money from the sale of corporate stocks. A person who owns a share of stock owns a part of the corporation.

A company's **board of directors** is elected by **stockholders**, or people who own shares in the corporation, and is the company's highest power. The board of directors usually votes on important decisions for the company.

Bill Lear works on a design for a Lear Jet.

something!" was his usual comment when discussions got too long. With his usual brash confidence, Lear decided to try something, and he bet millions of dollars that he knew more than all the top experts. At an age when many people are ready to retire, 60-year-old Bill Lear sold all his stock in his Michigan company and set up a business in Switzerland to make his small jet. With his usual impatience, though, he became irritated by delays in production and abruptly left Switzerland. Lear Jet, Incorporated, was established in Wichita, Kansas, in 1963.

Lear's willingness to gamble on his own genius struck many as a kind of madness. Banks and other investors refused to lend him money for his outrageous, unusual design. Marketing research people told him that company executives wanted luxury, and Lear was trying to sell them a plane so small that it had no walk-around space and no options. They explained that even if he were successful in building such a small-scale jet, no one would buy it. The entire demand for corporate jets in a market already overcrowded with competitors was expected to total 300 orders in the next seven years. That was not even close to what he would need to break even.

Lear took up the challenge in his usual intense, defiant way. Even though he had more than $8 million of his own money at stake, he gambled on setting up his production lines long before he had tested the parts he was producing. He worked seven days a week and personally involved himself in every department of the company. No experimental flight ever left the ground without Bill Lear at the controls or along for observation. He ordered design changes on the spot and demanded that engineers trim weight from pieces that were already as light as the men thought they could possibly make them. Employees began referring to pounds as "grandmothers" after Lear snarled that he would sell his own grandmother to save a pound on this airplane.

Lear Jet, Inc. won approval for its plane from the

Marketing research is done to find out what people want and the best way to satisfy their needs. **Surveys** are a common form of marketing research. Surveys are groups of questions that researchers ask a lot of people in order to gather their views and opinions. Marketing research is not foolproof, however, as Bill Lear proved.

A basic rule of business involves supply and demand. The number of products that are offered for sale at different prices at a certain time is called **supply**. **Demand** is the number of products that people are willing to buy at different prices at a certain time.

The Federal Aviation Administration is a government **regulatory agency**—an agency set up to regulate, or direct, business. The FAA determines whether a company may make aviation-related products and what rules the company must follow. Other federal regulatory agencies include the Environmental Protection Agency and the Equal Employment Opportunity Commission. The purpose of government regulation is to protect the public. For example, the FAA tests airplanes for safety, sets standards of safety and repairs for airlines, and investigates accidents involving airplanes.

Federal Aviation Administration within 18 months of starting work. It was a feat that astounded everyone in the aviation business, except Bill Lear. The eight-passenger Lear Jet was so light that it could fly at 560 miles per hour, saving executives hours of flying time. Yet because of standardized equipment and the savings in materials, the jet sold for about $640,000, almost half the price of other corporate planes.

Final satisfaction came when corporations lined up to buy Bill's "baby jets" as fast as he could make them. The Lear Jet made $52 million during its first year on the market. Now, just as Lear predicted, the skies are filled with tiny jets zooming corporate executives around the country.

Like the little train in the popular children's story, Lear accomplished things that no one expected because he believed he could do it. That determination changed the Lear Jet from an absurd impossibility into the little plane that could.

An Overpriced Popcorn

Orville Redenbacher

AFTER YEARS OF EATING POPCORN down to the bottom of the bowl and staring at a mound of unpopped kernels, Orville Redenbacher finally did something about it. His company developed an improved strain of popcorn that popped wide open and left almost no stragglers behind.

Certain that the public was tired of wasted popcorn and of cracking their teeth on partially popped popcorn, Redenbacher set out to sell his product. But no one was interested. Growers and processors took one look at the price and waved good-bye. As they saw it, people bought popcorn because it was good, cheap food. If someone could spend a lot of money on a snack, he or she would certainly buy something better than popcorn. Trying to sell an expensive gourmet popcorn was like selling gourmet oatmeal.

Opposite: Orville Redenbacher spent a lot of time in the cornfields, working to develop a fluffy popcorn.

At 63 years of age, Orville Redenbacher began to prove the doubters wrong.

Redenbacher's famous image as a rustic old-timer from the bygone era of rural life in the midwestern United States is no acting job. He was born on a 100-acre farm near Brazil, Indiana, in 1907. The youngest of four children, Orville helped with the family chores, milking cows on freezing winter nights and scrubbing hog houses in the heat of summer. None of the other Redenbacher children studied past the eighth grade in the local one-room school-house, but Orville was different. From a young age, he had been fascinated by books, and he achieved an impressive academic record. Not only was he the first in his family to graduate from high school, but he also was honored with an appointment to the United States Military Academy. An army career did not appeal to him, though. Redenbacher declined the honor and instead attended a school close to home—Purdue University in Lafayette, Indiana.

Despite his four years at a large university, Redenbacher remained a farm boy at heart. He spent one entire midwinter vacation working on a chicken farm to earn money to pay his school bills. Choosing agriculture as his major area of study, with plant breeding as his specialty, he graduated in 1928.

Redenbacher then returned home, where he tried to stay involved with both farming and education. First he taught farming courses at a local high school; later he took a job as a county agricultural

Orville Redenbacher

A farming **consolidation**, such as Redenbacher's Princeton Farms, consolidates, or unifies, several farms under one management or ownership.

agent. Not until 1940 did he venture into the business world. Orville was hired by a couple of businessmen who had bought several farms scattered around southwestern Indiana. His job was to organize and manage these 12,000 acres. Redenbacher handled the job so well that Princeton Farms grew into the largest consolidated farm in the state.

While organizing the farms, he often consulted with Charles Bowman, the manager of Purdue's Agricultural Alumni Seed Improvement Association. The two became good friends and eventually decided to start a business together. In 1951 they made their move. They bought a small company in Valparaiso, Indiana, that raised seed corn for animal feed.

Under Redenbacher's sound management, Princeton Farms grew into one of the largest farms in Indiana.

The two men were well matched. Redenbacher developed sound overall plans, and Bowman put the plans into action. They began to branch out into related farm products, such as grain bins, hoppers, and agricultural chemicals. Their best-seller was liquid fertilizer. Also on their list of products was popcorn seed.

Redenbacher was no stranger to popcorn, a fairly common Indiana crop. His father had eaten popcorn nearly every night, and Orville had acquired the same fondness for the snack. One of his projects while working for Princeton Farms had been to build a plant for drying popcorn. With his background in plant breeding, Redenbacher was naturally drawn to experimenting with ways to breed desirable characteristics into popcorn. In 1959 he hired a genetics expert in an attempt to develop a superior product.

In 1965 the company's genetic tinkering finally produced results: a product that popped up fluffier and more consistently than regular popcorn. For a popcorn lover like Redenbacher, it was hard to imagine that anyone would settle for less once they'd tried his product. The company got ready to produce this new brand of seed, which was called "Red Bow" popcorn.

But it seemed the time and money spent on research had all been wasted. The farmers who bought seed to grow popcorn weren't about to take a chance on the new product. Even if they had, processors wouldn't process it, and retailers wouldn't

In the popcorn business, the **processor** processes or prepares the corn so that it is ready to be used by consumers. The **retailer** buys the corn from the processor and sells it directly to consumers. One common retailer is a grocery store.

sell it. The problem was the price. No one could imagine consumers paying much for popcorn, no matter how good it was.

For four years, Redenbacher's sales pitch drew nothing but frowns and head shakes. In 1970, when Orville was 63 and in poor health, it appeared he would have to give up on his gourmet popcorn notion. As a last resort, he drove to Chicago to consult with a professional marketing agency. The consultants advised him to drop the Red Bow brand name, put a picture of his own face on the label, and advertise it as "Orville Redenbacher's Gourmet Popping Corn." As advertising experts later put it, Redenbacher had a unique "down-home, believable quality." His unforgettable name and his plain, out-of-date appearance (with his fondness for bow ties) made him a trusted symbol of honest, old-fashioned value.

Redenbacher began producing his popcorn himself, and his product did gain a small but loyal following in specialty stores. Among its admirers was Blue Plate Foods, a New Orleans subsidiary of the giant Hunt-Wesson food corporation. Blue Plate Foods worked out a deal to distribute the product in the southern United States. As part of the agreement, Redenbacher took the starring role in promoting his popcorn. In contrast to the slick, glamorous, supercool spokespersons for most products, the plain, honest Orville stood out, and he attracted buyers. From sales of around 300,000 pounds in 1970-71,

Blue Plate Foods is a subsidiary of Hunt-Wesson. A **subsidiary** is a corporation that is controlled by a **parent company** (like Hunt-Wesson) which owns the majority of the subsidiary's stock.

Getting popcorn from one part of the country to another is called **distribution**—making sure a product is at the right place at the right time. The product may go directly from the manufacturer to the consumer, or it may go from the manufacturer to a store (a retailer) and then to the consumer.

Redenbacher's volume of business grew to more than 5 million pounds by 1975-76.

Redenbacher was nearing 70 years of age. Neither he nor his partner had children who were interested in taking over the business. He did not care to take on the problems of a large corporation. His continuing role as spokesman for the popcorn that bears his name gives the impression that he's still in charge of the operation. In fact, he sold the last of his interests in his gourmet popcorn to the Hunt-Wesson group in 1976.

Ironically, although he is one of the most recognized people in the food industry, Orville Redenbacher made more money selling liquid fertilizer than he ever did from his popcorn. He did not get the best possible deal when he sold his popcorn business.

Meanwhile, with Orville Redenbacher working strictly as a hired actor promoting the product (he claims that he provides only the hot air while others provide the corn!), his gourmet popcorn has shattered the scornful predictions first made for it. Despite its high price tag, it has become the best-selling brand of popcorn in the world.

Promotion is all of a company's selling activities, including advertising, face-to-face selling, and special efforts such as coupons or contests. Orville Redenbacher promotes his popcorn for the Hunt-Wesson company by appearing in advertisements and making special appearances.

A Fly-By-Night Scheme That Worked

Federal Express

Frederick Smith

Most OF US HAVE RECEIVED, AT SOME time or other, a grade that we thought was lower than we deserved. We may have argued with the teacher about it or just grumbled to our friends. Frederick W. Smith found a unique way to handle that kind of situation. He decided to try out the ideas he'd proposed in a research paper that had been graded harshly by his professor. That term paper laid the groundwork for an overnight delivery service that dramatically improved the speed at which small packages could be delivered. When his delivery service earned millions of dollars, Smith had ample proof that his rejected ideas had been misjudged by the professor.

Frederick Smith was born in Marks, Mississippi, in 1944. His father was a millionaire known as the

"Bus King" of the South because of the bus service he had built from scratch. Despite the family's wealth, Fred's childhood was anything but easy. His father died when Fred was four. The boy also suffered from a bone disease that kept him from running and playing during most of his early years.

One of Smith's greatest thrills was flying airplanes, and he earned his pilot's license at the age of 15. Smith first developed his idea for making money from his interest in aircraft while studying at Yale University in New Haven, Connecticut. When he researched a paper for an economics course, he discovered that the United States had never come up with a good system for rapidly delivering small packages, especially to small cities and towns. Companies in smaller communities were at a disadvantage because they could not get service as quickly as those in major cities. Overnight delivery of packages was almost unknown.

Smith decided that the problem could never be solved using existing airlines and depots. For one thing, the first priority of existing airlines was passenger service, and all attempts at package delivery had to fit in with those schedules. Smith came up with a radical new proposal. Why not bypass the existing air routes entirely? Why not set up an air delivery service with a single package-sorting center that would serve the entire country?

Smith's paper drew a cool response from his professor. He was told that the proposal was all

The computer and electronic **industries** refers to the group of computer and electronic manufacturers as a whole. The word *industry* can also be use more generally to mean all of a nation's manufacturing activity.

wrong, and he received a mediocre grade for his effort. It wasn't an unusual experience for him since, as he has admitted, he was not a good student. But he was convinced that, despite what his teacher thought, the idea would work. Smith realized that U.S. business needs were changing. Many companies had moved out of urban areas and were no longer served by the passenger airlines. New industries such as computers and electronics also depended on rapid delivery of parts.

After graduating from Yale in 1966, Smith put his flying experience to use in the armed forces. He flew more than 200 combat missions in Vietnam before leaving the service in 1970. Using some of his inherited money, he then bought Little Rock Airmotive, a small company in Arkansas. The company, which specialized in aircraft modification, was just a stepping-stone on Smith's way to the grand design he had outlined in his Yale research paper. His next move was to hire researchers to study whether his idea had a chance of succeeding. The results indicated that it could work.

In 1972, at the age of 28, Fred Smith was ready to challenge the odds and the skeptics in one of the boldest gambles that the business world has ever seen. First he obtained certification for his company, Federal Express, as an air taxi service. That meant he could fly to any airport in the country. Next he needed to choose the hub—the collection point for all the packages flown in from around the country.

Memphis, where he had spent his youth, had everything he was looking for. It was located near the center of the country and had mild winter weather. Equally important, the Memphis airport was getting far less traffic than it was built to handle, so it would welcome the fleets of planes that Smith would bring in. Smith was given space in the airport terminal, as well as a lease on some abandoned Air Force hangars.

That was the easy part. Smith's plan called for airplanes to fly into Memphis every evening with packages collected from 100 cities. The packages were sorted in Memphis, and the planes would return to their home cities with new packages that same night. In each city the packages were sorted more closely, and trucks headed out to deliver each package to its final destination. This system required many planes, as well as pilots to fly them and people to maintain them. In order to guarantee fast delivery in smaller communities, Smith needed his own fleet of delivery trucks and employees for sorting, delivery, and management. Though independently wealthy, Fred Smith couldn't finance such a costly operation by himself. Somehow he would have to persuade other people to invest over $70 million in an untried project that some said could never work.

Smith researched every angle of the business so that he could answer any questions about its workability, and then he turned on the charm. In what one business analyst called the greatest sales

A Federal Express package is flown into Memphis, where it is sorted (top). *The package is then flown to its destination city* (center), *sorted again and driven to its final destination* (bottom).

feat of all time, Smith found all the investors he needed. He did so even though potential investors had a lot of doubts about his plan. After purchasing 25 French passenger jets and converting them to his own cargo specifications, Smith was ready to begin the great experiment.

The first evening of business, April 17, 1973, strongly supported the Yale professor's opinion. As Smith looked on anxiously, his Federal Express planes brought in a total of only 18 packages. And things got worse over the next few months. The Arab oil embargo caused oil prices to soar, driving up the cost of fuel. Smith's Arkansas company became mired in legal problems in a dispute over taxes. Money was so tight for Federal Express that Smith's pilots occasionally had to use their personal credit cards to buy fuel for their planes.

Beset by all these problems and costs, Smith had to turn to investors for more money. Few of them, however, were willing to throw additional money into a business that had lost $24 million in just two years. Most air freight experts had come to share the professor's opinion: Smith was doomed to failure. They pointed out the terrible inefficiency of his system: A package sent from San Francisco to San Diego would have to go thousands of miles out of its way to Memphis before reaching its destination. With the high cost of fuel, Federal Express could not afford those extra miles. Smith got the $11

About 60 percent of the world's known oil supply is in the Middle East and North Africa. In 1973, a number of the nations which own the oil imposed an oil embargo on Western nations. An **embargo** is a ban on exports of certain products. (An **export** is a product that is sent to a foreign country to be sold.) When the Middle Eastern countries reduced sales of oil to the U.S., oil prices in the U.S. rose dramatically.

An important part of the U.S. business system is the use of credit. **Credit** is the ability to get goods or services in exchange for a promise to pay later. A popular way of describing credit is the saying "Buy now, pay later." Banks play an important role in the credit system. People place the money they have saved in a bank. The bank pays the person **interest**, a payment for the use of the person's money. The bank then loans money to businesses, which eventually pay back the money plus an interest payment. The **interest rate** measures how much the interest payment will be. It is measured as a percentage of the money loaned. For example, if a bank loans you $100 at a 10 percent interest rate, you will have to pay the bank back $100 plus 10 percent of $100, or $10, for a total of $110.

million he needed to stay in business only by agreeing to pay a high interest rate and by giving the investors hundreds of thousands of shares of company stock.

Smith clung to his idea that as long as he could guarantee next-day delivery, business would improve. By the end of 1975, Federal Express was finally taken seriously. The company handled more than 12,000 packages per night that year. Large companies, in particular, had begun to realize the value of immediate delivery. A year later, the total passed 20,000 per night, more than Smith's fleet of 48 planes could carry.

The obvious solution to this welcome problem was to use larger planes. But federal aviation rules stated that planes used for air taxi service could carry loads of no more than 7,500 pounds. Although he was opposed by the major airlines, Smith persuaded Congress to abolish that rule in 1977. By 1978 Federal Express was processing over 35,000 packages per night. Gross earnings grew to more than $15 million per month.

Federal Express has since become a corporation employing more than 50,000 employees and delivering roughly 150 million packages per year. But perhaps the greatest compliment to Fred Smith's genius is that his "hub and spokes" routing system has been copied by passenger airlines, as well as air freight competitors. All of this gives Smith an A+ in the business world, even if it comes too late to change his college term paper grade.

For Further Reading...

Bryant, K.L., Jr. and Dethloff, H.C. *A History of American Business*. Prentice-Hall Inc., 1983.

Clary, D.C. *Great American Brands*. Fairchild Books, 1981.

Fucini, J.J. and Fucini, S. *Entrepreneurs: The Men and Women Behind Famous Brand Names*. G.K. Hall, 1985.

Livesay, H.C. *American Made: Men Who Shaped the American Economy*. Little, Brown & Company, 1980.

Moskowitz, M., Katz, M. and Levering, R., eds. *Everybody's Business*. Harper and Row, 1980.

Slappey, S.G. *Pioneers of American Business*. Grosset & Dunlap, 1970.

Sobel, R. and Sicilia, D.B. *The Entrepreneurs: An American Adventure*. Houghton Mifflin Company, 1986

Thompson, J. *The Very Rich Book*. William Morrow & Company, 1981.

Vare, E. and Ptacek, G. *Mothers of Invention: From the Bra to the Bomb: Forgotten Women and Their Unforgettable Ideas*. William Morrow & Company, 1988.

INDEX

Words in **boldface** are defined in the text.

Hoskins, Ruth, 40
Hunt-Wesson corporation, 67-68

I

incorporate, definition of, 58
industrialization, definition of, 13
industry, definition of, 71
interest, definition of, 75
interest rate, definition of, 75

J

Jell-O, 6-9

K

Kornei, Otto, 48

L

The Landlord's Game, 39-40
Lear, Incorporated, 58
Lear jet, 55-61
Lear Jet, Incorporated, 59
Lear, William, 55-61
Little Rock Airmotive, 71

M

Magie, Elizabeth, 39-40, 44
Majestic radio, 57
marketing, definition of, 33
marketing research, definition of, 60
mass production, definition of, 16
Milbank, Jeremiah, 22
Monopoly game, 36-44, 80
Motorola, 57

N

Nabisco, 10
New York Condensed Milk Company, 22
New York Public Library, 27, 48
nonprofit organization, definition of, 46

O

Orville Redenbacher popcorn, 2, 63-68

P

parent company, definition of, 67
Parker Brothers, 37-44
Parker, Charles, 42
Parker, George, 42, 44
patent, definition of, 20
Pennsylvania Temperance Society, 13
photoconductivity, 48
photocopiers, 45-53
popcorn, 63-68
Postum Company, 34
Princeton Farms, 65
processor, definition of, 66
profit, definition of, 46
promotion, definition of, 68
Purdue University, 64, 65

Q

quick-freezing, 29-35
Quincy Radio Laboratories, 56

R

radio frequency amplifier, 58
Reader's Digest, 23-28

"Red Bow" popcorn, 66
Redenbacher, Orville, 2, 62-68
regulatory agency, definition of, 61
"Remember the Alamo!", 18
research, definition of, 48
retailer, definition of, 66
risks, 23
royalty payments, definition of, 51

S

Selenyi, Paul, 48
Shakers, 20-21
Smith, Frederick W., 69-75
stocks, definition of, 39
stockholder, definition of, 58
stock market crash of 1929, 39
subsidiary, definition of, 67
supply, definition of, 60
survey, definition of, 60

T

Temperance Society, *see* Pennsylvania
    Temperance Society
"10-22-38 ASTORIA," 48-49
"Terraqueous Wagon," 18
"Treatise of Bread and Breadmaking," 15

V

vacuum pan, 20-21

W

Wait, Pearl, 7
Wallace, DeWitt, 23-28
Wallace, Lila Acheson, *see* Acheson, Lila Bell

Webb Publishing Company, 24-25
Westinghouse Electric, 26
Woodward, Orator, 7-8
World War I, 25
World War II, 35, 50, 58

X

xerography, 51
Xerox Corporation, 45-53
Xerox photocopier, 45-53

An 1890s photograph of the Salem, Massachusetts building where Monopoly is still made today.

ACKNOWLEDGEMENTS

The photographs and illustrations in this book are reproduced through the courtesy of: pp. 1, 54, 57, 59, 61, Learjet Corporation; p. 2, Daniel J. Edelman, Inc.; pp. 6, 8, 29, 31, 34, 35, General Foods Corporate Archives; p. 10, Nabisco Brands, Inc.; p. 12, Kent Memorial Library, Suffield, Connecticut; p. 14, The Library of Congress; pp. 17, 19, 21 (bottom), 22, Borden, Inc.; p. 21 (top), Collection of The United Society of Shakers, Sabbathday Lake, Maine; pp. 24, 27, 28, *Reader's Digest*; p. 25, C.P. Gibson—Minnesota Historical Society; pp. 37, 43, 44, 80, Parker Brothers; p. 38, National Archives; pp. 49, 50, 52, 53, Xerox Corporation; pp. 62, 64, Beatrice/Hunt-Wesson; p. 65, Princeton Farms; pp. 69, 73, Federal Express Corporation. Cover illustration by Stephen Clement.